Who Is Destroying
The Black Race
In America?

Who Is Destroying The Black Race In America?

iUniverse, Inc.
New York   Bloomington

Who Is Destroying The Black Race in America?

Copyright © 2006 by Ricky D. Carraway

iUniverse books may be ordered through booksellers or by contacting:

iUniverse
1663 Liberty Drive
Bloomington, IN 47403

www.iuniverse.com
1-800-Authors (1-800-288-4677)

Because of the dynamic nature of the Internet, any Web addresses or links contained in this book may have changed since publication and may no longer be valid.

ISBN: 978-0-595-41590-8 (pbk)
ISBN: 978-0-595-85938-2 (ebk)

Printed in the United States of America

iUniverse rev. date: 12/17/2008

CONTENTS

PREFACE

This book is written to foster a desire, establish clear understanding, and restore the needed confidence back into the life of the black family in America. However, it does not address every concern of the black race. It does look at some events of slavery, the Jim-Crow Era, voters' rights, self-induced afflictions, and personal responsibility. After looking into historical writings, research data, and personal interviews, I wanted to write something that would shine light on some of the conditions for the black race in America that could help reestablish a firm foundation, build self-esteem, and create a bridge to encourage black families to cross over and take positions in life as partakers of wealth and abundance of this nation. Before the bridge can be built and we cross over it, some tearing down must be done. Before a seed can properly be planted into the earth, the soil must be tilled to remove anything that would hinder growth. If the black family is going to prevail, it must embrace the meaning of this concept

HISTORY OF THE BLACK RACE

To understand the present conditions of the black family in America, we must first go back and look at some of the historical facts of what the black family went through during pre-slavery and slavery in America and beyond. There are no blacks alive today that were around during those harsh and unpleasant years, but history affords us the opportunity to go through its record of events.

Cited in wikipedia.org, the history of *slavery in the United States* (1619-1865) began soon after English colonists first settled Virginia and lasted until the passage of the Thirteenth Amendment to the U.S. Constitution.

Many slaves were transported out of Africa, according to an article in slavevoyages.org " when the trans-Atlantic slave trade ended in 1867, over 12 million Africans had been forcibly relocated. Though little trace is left of the individual histories of these displaced peoples, thousands of records remain of the voyages that brought them. That gave the general public a chance to rediscover the reality of one of the largest movements of people in world history (slavevoyages.org).

Despite the slave initiatives against blacks at Jamestown VA, slavery did not begin with America. In about.com the following statements were made:

When Europeans arrived along the West African coast; slavery already existed on the continent. However, in his book The African Slave Trade, Basil Davidson points out that slavery in Africa and the brutal form of slavery that would develop in the Americas were vastly different. African slavery was more akin to European serfdom -- the condition of most Europeans in the 15th century. In the Ashanti Kingdom of West Africa, for example, slaves could marry, own property, and even own slaves. And slavery ended after a certain number of years of servitude. Most importantly, African slavery was never passed from one generation to another, and it lacked the racist notion that whites were masters and blacks were slaves (about.com au).

Historian's account of conditions with blacks brought to Jamestown Virginia.

Cited in an article on henryburke1010 tripod.com in 1640, three indentured servants, one black, and two white, fled from a Virginia plantation. When caught and returned to their owner, the two white servants had their indenture extended for four years. The black servant, named John Punch, was sentenced to serve his said master or his assigns for the time of his natural life. John Punch's status was changed from an indentured servant to a slave. It is not difficult to imagine how rapidly it became an accepted practice to accuse black indentured servants of infractions falsely in order to keep them enslaved for life. In 1650, Anthony was one of four hundred Africans in the Virginia Colony among a white settler population of nearly 19,000. In Virginia County, where Johnson lived, twenty or so African men and women were free, and thirteen of this number owned their own homes. But a drastic change loomed in the near future for Africans who were brought to Virginia! In 1661, the enslavement of black Africans was legalized in Virginia (The Afro-American newspaper)

Slavery timeline of events cited by nps.gov:

1630   Indications by surviving wills, inventories, deeds and other documents that in some instances it was considered "customary practice to hold some Negroes in a form of life service." It should be noted that by examining these documents it was also found that some blacks were able to hold on to their status of being indentured servants, thus, eventually gaining their freedom.

1639   All persons except Negroes are to be with Arms and Ammunition.

1640   John Punch, a runaway indentured Servant, first documented slave for life.

1662   Slavery was recognized in the statutory law of the colony.

       Legislation was passed defining the status of mulatto children. Children would Be considered the same status as the mother. If the child was born to a slave, the Child would be considered a slave.

1667   Baptism does not bring freedom. Until the General Assembly outlawed it, baptism could be the grounds for a black slave to obtain his/her freedom. It was considered for a period of time that it was not proper for a Christian to enslave a fellow Christian.

1670   Blacks or Indians could no longer own white indentured servants.

1680   An act was passed preventing insurrections among slaves. Blacks could not congregate in large numbers for supposed funeral or feasts. Blacks must also obtain written authorization to leave a plantation at any given time. They could not remain at another plantation longer than 4 hours.

1691   First act prohibiting intermarriage.

       No Negro or Mulatto may be set free by any person unless the pay for the Transportation out of the colony within six months or forfeit ten pounds of sterling so that the church wardens might have the Negro transported.

1692   Negroes must give up ownership of horses, cattle or hogs.

       Separate courts for the trial of slaves charged with a capital crime, thus depriving them of the right of a trial by jury.

1700   Slaves composed half of Virginia's un-free labor force.

1705   Slave laws were codified. (nps.gov na)

The life of the Negro slave experienced one of the most inhumane treatments of a people in the history of man. Much of that treatment existed in various parts of the world, even at the hands of other Negroes. Help would come through a reconstruction period.

The Reconstruction Era was a period of time that favored freedom for Negroes, but that freedom would come at a cost, a fight between the northern and southern states in the union. As cited in an article in pbs.com The Rise and Fall of Jim Crow:

President Andrew Johnson alienated Congress with his Reconstruction policy. He supported white supremacy in the South and favored pro-Union Southern political leaders who had aided the Confederacy once war had been declared. Southerners, with Johnson's support, attempted to restore slavery in substance if not in name. In 1866, Congress and President Johnson battled for control of Reconstruction. The Congress won. Northern voters gave a smashing victory -- more than two-thirds of the seats in Congress -- to the Radical Republicans in the 1866 congressional election, enabling Congress to control Reconstruction and override any vetoes that Johnson might impose. Congress passed the Reconstruction Acts of 1867 that divided the Confederate states (except for Tennessee, which had been re-admitted to the Union) into five military districts. Each state was required to accept the Thirteenth and Fourteenth Amendments to the Constitution, which granted freedom and political rights of blacks.

Each Southern state had to incorporate these requirements into their constitutions, and blacks were empowered with the vote. Yet, Congress failed to secure land for blacks, thus allowing whites to economically control blacks. The Freedmen's Bureau was authorized to administer the new laws and help blacks attain their economic, civil, educational, and political rights. The newly created state governments were generally Republican in character and were governed by political coalitions of blacks, Northerners who had migrated to the South (called "carpetbaggers" by Southern Democrats), and Southerners who allied with the blacks and carpetbaggers (referred to as "scalawags" by their opponents). This uneasy coalition of black and white Republicans passed significant civil rights legislation in many states. Courts were reorganized, judicial procedures improved, and public school systems established. Segregation existed but it was flexible. But as blacks slowly progressed, white Southerners resented their achievements and their empowerment, even though they were in a political minority in every state but South Carolina. (Richard Wormser)

Newly formed white militias, such as the Ku Klux Klan (KKK), resisted the freedom for blacks. According to an article in the Spartcus Educational: The first branch of the Ku Klux Klan was established in Pulaski, Tennessee, in May, 1866. A year later, a general organization of local Klans was established in Nashville in April 1867. Most of the leaders were former members of the Confederate Army and the first Grand Wizard was Nathan Forrest, an outstanding general during the American War. During the next two years Klansmen wearing masks, white cardboard hats and draped in white sheets, tortured and killed black Americans and sympathetic whites. Immigrants, who they blamed for the election of Radical Republicans, were also targets of their hatred. Between 1868 and 1870, the Ku Klux Klan played an important role in restoring white rule in North Carolina, Tennessee and Georgia (John Simkin). The KKK was dedicated to using violence in any manner to deter blacks from achieving equality.

The name Ku Klux Klan has since been used by many independent groups opposing the Cilvil Rights Movements and desegrigation especially in the 1950s and 1960s. During this period, they often acted with impunity by alliances with Southern police departments, as during the reign of Bull Connor in Birmingham Alabama; or governor's offices, as with George Wallace of Alabama. (wikipedia. com)

Civil rights groups were instrumental in fighting for the rights of blacks during the 1950s and even in today's society. These groups focus on abolishing discrimination by race and other physical aspects. Groups such as NAACP, SCLC, ACLU, COFC, CORE, and many others continue to be on the front line defending civil rights.

Civil rights gains came mostly through the unity of blacks along with the help of many whites; there was a sense of urgency and loyalty that kept the black race knitted together, and a since of fairness that moved some whites to fight for equal rights for blacks. Blacks of today seem not as concerned with the discipline and unity that existed in the past. There is a vast difference between blacks' uniting together during Martin Luther King era as opposed to during the twenty-first century, and quite a difference in the behavior of black men and women willing to make sacrifices for the whole of their race.

You've heard it said that men are the head of the family, which is true for most cultures, especially in the black family unit. But that trend has been evaporating through social decline and dysfunctional minds.

According to Wikipedia .org, on single parents:
Today in the United States, being raised by a single parent is not uncommon. About three in ten children live in a single parent home. The most common type of single parent homes are one's with only a mother. However, single father are the fastest growing type of family situations. The number of single fathers has risen by 60% in the last ten years alone. There has been a 280% increase among Whites and 543% increase among African Americans in singleparent families over the past 40 years" (Bianchi, 1995, U.S. Bureau of the Census, 1993).

More black women are becoming the head of their households because of the "unstable and eroding relationship." Not only are black women becoming head of their households, but if you think about it , you will find that black women play a major role in the black race, because without her, more black children would end up in foster homes.

The black family is slowly being destroyed, because black men and women have become gun slingers, fighting and shooting each other with separations and divorce grievance, which is an enemy against the sanctity of marriage. If children are involved, this puts mental challenges in their way for the rest of their lives.

Many counter-productive power decision are made by the court, which rules according to the law, but not necessary in the best interest of all partyies involved. While it is the responsibility of both parents to provide for their children, the way the courts handle the governing of the responsibilities, they can take away forty-five to fifty percent of income from the non-custodial parent. There are not many people, including the judges themselves, who can live off forty-five to fifty percent of their income, especially when the income of both parents is not adequate. There are many instances when marriages are in a repairable state, but the enticement from the monetary amount the custodian parent can receive is enough to encourage any frail marriage to break up.

It is no secret that the black race has been discriminated against in our society when it comes to being fully accepted and having intricate roles in our nation's economy, especially at the senior corporate levels in private sectors and government. There has been undeniable progress in many areas. Nevertheless, the evidence is overwhelming that the problems Affirmative Action seeks to address -- widespread discrimination, exclusion, and their ripple effects -- continue to exist.

An article in clinton2.nara title Justification For Affirmative Action shows:

- Two pairs of male testers visited the offices of a nationally franchised employment agency on two different days. The black tester in each pair received no job referrals. In contrast, the white testers who appeared minutes later were interviewed by the agency, coached on interviewing techniques, and referred to and offered jobs as switchboard operators.
- A black female tester applied for employment at a major hotel chain in Virginia where she was told that she would be called if they wished to pursue her application. Although she never received a call, her equally qualified white counterpart appeared a few minutes later, was told about a vacancy for a front desk clerk, later interviewed, and offered the job.
- A black male tester asked about an ad for a sales position at a Maryland car dealership. He was told that the way to enter the business would be to start by washing cars. However, his white counterpart, with identical credentials, was immediately interviewed for the sales job.

- A suburban Maryland company advertised for a typist/ receptionist. When a black tester applied for the position, she was interviewed but heard nothing further. When an identically qualified white tester was interviewed, the employer offered her a better position that paid more than the receptionist job and that provided tuition assistance. Follow up calls by the black tester elicited no response even though the white tester refused the offer.
- A GAO audit study uncovered significant discrimination against Hispanic testers. Hispanic testers received 25 percent fewer job interviews, and 34 percent fewer job offers than other testers. In one glaring example of discrimination, a Hispanic tester was told that a "counter help" job at a lunch service company had been filled. Two hours later, an Anglo tester was offered the job (Clinton 2.nara)

Enpowerment is needed in the black community, but must first be preceeded by self-control, determination, and the spirit of excellence to help combat discrimation.

THE ROLE OF THE BLACK MAN

Life itself beckons the black man to stand up, and time will pass you by if you don't take it seriously. When seasons change, time doesn't ask for permission. Black men are in positions to have a greater motivational push than any other race in Amerivca. Black men are not on the bottom and not on the top, but in the middle, which is a place where we can see where we need to go.

When Bill Cosby speaks about the conditions of the black family, many blacks become defensive and stir up strife and lash out at him. I would like to congratulate Mr. Cosby for taking a courageous stance against ignorance and apathy concerning the conditions of the black race. He encourages us to strive for excellence. However, the opinions of people like Rev. Jesse Peterson (Founder and President of BOND, the Brotherhood Organization of a New Destiny) are a clear example of astract information driving on a one-way street. His negative views of the black race are one-sided, and he blames the condition of black people solely upon their being lazy. The pathway to redemption must be included in every act of criticism. There must be a clear direction to redeem oneself, as well as ways of addressing the correct problems that exist. Black males must resist the actions that cause one to go to prison.

According to Dec 31, 2004 US Department of Justice Statistics:

At year end 2004 there were 3,218 black male sentenced prison inmates per 100,000 black males in the United States, compared to

1,220 Hispanic male inmates per 100,000 Hispanic males and 463 white male inmates per 100,000 white males. (ojp.usdoj.gov/bjs)

Some of the disparity between the number of black men in jail verses white and Hispanics relates to a different standard of justice by the court. Yet still, far too many black men are too quick to embrace the militant view, which in reality points more to the use of muscle than brains. It also says that they don't have the ability or drive to reach goals, so they should take a position that feeds into having a victim mentality and settle for achievement as a street hussler. If one is lost in the woods, that person can sit down and engage in a pitty party and feel helpless, or they can think like a wildernessman and try climbing trees to see if they can see the direction out of the woods. Life on the streets is more difficult and less rewarding than life that influences one to finish school, go to college, and tap into one's potential to become a success.

The role of the black man and women is quite remarkable, they both has tasted the bitterness of opression through enslavement, as well as the harshness of classism, and yet has still survived. The greatest obstacle facing the black man today is not what people think of him, but rather what he thinks of himself. Even during times of enslavement, the black man knew some things that his slave masters knew, he heard what was spoken, and saw what was done. The problem was the black man was not allowed to do or say what he had learned; that is why we find it so difficult to follow through with ideals and desires. In a sense, we are still waiting for permission to live. They say if you keep a dog tied up for a long period of time, and later untie him, the dog will not go to far beyond the distance of the rope that bound him, even though he is free. Our white brothers have found new ways to live and profit, and owning slaves are over for them. Now it is time for being owned to be over for us. The Constitution can say we are endowed with such inalienable rights and that all men are created equal, but it is up to each individual to use his creative abilities. Too many black men have picked up the axe and, insted of using it to chop their way out of the jungle of life's challenges, they have turned and used it on each other.

According to the author of *My Black Crime Problem, and Ours,* John J. DiIulio, Jr:

Based on its latest crime victimization surveys, the U.S. Bureau of Justice Statistics estimates that in 1993 alone blacks committed 1.29 million violent crimes against other blacks—80 percent of all violent crimes against blacks. Blacks also committed 1.54 million violent crimes against whites—18 percent of all violent crimes against whites. As a number of analysts have begun to notice, blacks are about 50 times more likely to commit violent crimes against whites than whites are to commit violent crimes against blacks. Like the Sentencing Project's "1 in 3" number, this "50 to 1" statistic is technically correct. If you divide the total number of black-on-white violent crimes in 1993 (1.29 million) by the number of black males age 20 to 29 in the population in 1993 (3.94 million), you get a ratio equal to 1,013 violent crimes against whites per 10,000 young black males. 7.8 percent of crime on blacks represents black on black crime, as opposeed to 17 percent being white on black crimes. (John J. DiIulio Jr)

Many of the problems affecting the black male are manefested out of drugs which lure him into other criminal activities, causing harm to himself and others. Crimes of this nature can be avoided through early intervention programs, which can be ministered through faith-based inititives and community involvment groups; either way, blacks must get involved with finding solutions. We have blamed the white race, the Jews, Latinos, and now the Mexicans for things they don't control in our lives. No man can control your will, desire, and atttitude. These atributes come from within, and they must be established as well as launched from within. If mankind can find a way to go to the moon and build submarines and live underwater, surely we can overcome the obstacles that stand in our way to a successful life for ourselves. When a man consentrates too much on himself, all he sees is where he is presently, which may not be a comfortable place, so all he thinks about is motivated from a point of doom and gloom. Black men must not judge where they're going by immediate circumstances, for they do not dictate where black men are going.

Washington Post columnist, April 11, 2005, *The gains of the last 40 years:*

Have created a new, larger, stronger black middle class. Many young black men lack a clear understanding of the proper steps that lead to manhood and the responsibilities that go with them. (William Raspberry)

When it comes to knowing how to be productive men, we don't need to reinvent the wheel. The roads have already been paved. It takes a sense of reponsibility in order to meet responsibilities. There are plenty of role models to give advice.

The most recent report by The Center For American Progress states:

> The unemployment rate among black teens stood at 37 percent - more than double the rate for white teens. Their schooling is weak, and the labor market places more value than it use to on reading and math skills. As a result, many young black men turned to illegal activity – especially the drug trade – in the 1980s and early 1990s. But while crime rates finally fell during the latter 1990s, our prison populations kept rising. We now have two million people locked up on any given day in the U.S. – over two-thirds of whom are minority men. By some estimates, nearly 30 percent of all young black men have already been in prison at some point. (Harry j Holzer)

Whatever you commit yourself to is what you will become successful in; if you commit yourself to using drugs, you will be successful and achieve status as a drug addict. If you commit yourself to breaking laws, you will be successful and achieve status as a criminal; but if you commit yourself to staying focused and going to school, you will be successful and achieve status as a graduate. If you commit to nothing, you will become nothing, but to if you commit to something you will become something. Criminal activity is the doorway that leads to life as a criminal, and whatever other doors you walk through will lead you to what is behind it.

The greatest act that will change the kind of life that the black race will live is the act of black men and women taking responsibility. Far too many black men are geared up when it comes to chasing women, making babies, and being militant, but geared down when it comes to taking care of their children and too many black women accepts unacceptable behavioral from their men, by not demanding they be responsible. The state and local government realizes that it can not tolerate those of us who refuse to adhere to the laws of the land, so it is identifying those whom it must separate from in order to protect people who are productive and law abiding. To facilitate this separation more prisons are being built and more enforcement officers are being hired.

According to BBC News, April 2006 figures:

The 50 US states along with the District of Columbia and the federal government held as many as 1,355,748 people as of June last year, Another 665,475 inmates were under lock and key in municipal and local jails. In total, one in every 142 people living in the United States was in jail last year. (Matthew Davis)

One thing about the leaders in our society is that they don't have any remorse for locking up criminals. If you don not want to go to jail, stay out of trouble because they will carry out that responsibility to the fullest.

Black men need not fear jails, for to go to jail is a choice; you must qualify by breaking the law in order to go. It is like a test that you must pass to get in. Society can produce jails, drugs, guns, and child pornography, but it can't make a person participate in them. That comes only by being drawn into them by your own lust.

There are too many black men unaware of how successful they really can become and how their contributions can enhance the life of others. One can never truly know who they are and what their mission is until they get in touch with the one who made them. It takes knowledge of God to be able to have knowledge of yourself. To deny God will only lead to a life filled with illusions and emptiness and a void that can never be filled. There are more testimonies in church about people who have overcome a troubled life than any other institution in the world. The Center for Faith-Based and Community Initiatives (CFBCI) welcomes the participation of faith-based and community organizations as essential partners in assisting our country's neediest citizens. The power to transform a life is real, alive, and available through none other then Jesus Christ, and there are millions upon millions of people who will attest to this fact. Some people are just too cool for God and feel they don't need anyone to legislate their life and thus reject any intervention or acknowledgment of Him; yet every day of their life the evidence of God is all around them.

Black men yearn to have respect, authority, recognition, power, money, and love, just like all men, and there is nothing wrong with those desires, but in order to have something different from what you have, you must do something different from what you are doing. We must see ourselves as coworkers with other brothers of the world. They are not our enemies, but just simply men trying to get ahead and be the best at what they do. To get ahead is a possibility for all men, but the odds favor the ones whose minds are prepared and ready. If black men allow themselves to be destroyed, then it is they who are destroying the black race. The roles of black men are to be strong, wise, intelligent, faithful, righteous, family-oriented and Godly. When this happens, his ways will be clear and unstoppable. His race will be accepted and in demand, and, like Dr Martin Luther King Jr. said, one day his children will be judged by the contents of their character and not by the color of their skin. There will always be people who will think that black people are inferior and will not accept us regardless of how successful we are. Senator Barack Obama has been attacked by many based on his skin color. Barack's running for President was difficult for many blacks to accept. Often, blacks that have accumulated great wealth find it difficult to embrace other blacks. Bob Johnson, founder of Black Entertainment Television (BET), spoke very negatively against Senator Obama. Until black men decide to work together in unity, our struggles will lead us nowhere. We have been fighting an uphill battle against the system for so long, we should be pretty good at it by now. If we use our abilities to fight the system as we fight each other, we could live a more prosperous life in this age.

The Nation of Islam under the leadership of the Honorable Minister Louis Farrakhan is the catalyst for the growth and development of Islam in America. Although I do not embrace the Muslim religion, Minister Farrakhan has instilled a sense of self-respect and dignity into the lives of many black men, including freedom from drugs, alcohol, and self-destructive life styles. Every black man should be a member of a black culture awareness organization to help strengthen and clarify his obligation to himself and others. This could help him stay true to his role as a black man.

THE ROLE OF THE BLACK WOMEN

Many black women are pulling more than their share of the load when it comes to responsibilities in the home and taking care of the children. Had it not been that black women traditionaly kept her children with her when their father walk out, more black children would had ended up in ophan homes than there were.

Abortion was not a consideration in most black homes, and was shamful to even mention. In todays era, the number of black babies being aborted is staggering.

According to a article in Black genocide.org:

Blacks make up about 12 percent of the population in the United States but account for 32 percent of the abortions; and about 1,450 black infants are aborted everyday in the United States (Clinard H. Childress Jr.).

It is not to say that abortions are the results of ill marriage, but it does speak to the role of black women.

Ebony Nov 23, 2004, article *Shocking State of Black Marriages:* The number of Black married couples is only half the number of married Whites, and the situation is getting worse. In 1963 when Dr. Martin Luther King Jr. gave his "I Have a Dream" speech, more than 70 percent of all Black families were headed by married couples. In 2002 that number was 48 percent. An even more alarming statistic is the increase in the number of both Black men and women who have never been married. Nearly 45 percent of Black men have never married and 42 percent of Black women have never married. More to the point, an increasing number of Black women will never get married. The percentage of Black women who are married declined from 62 percent to 31 percent between 1950 and 2002 (Bennett Kinnon).

The black women has a very important and significant role to play in today's society. There were times when it seemed like the black women had energizing power like the sun. They could entice their men to see where they were going, increase their strength, give them hope for tomorrow and plant the seed of determination in them so deeply that they became grounded, rooted, and yeilded great ambition. The roles of black women have always been many; she has to be a strong nurture and hard worker, and yet still be romantic. Many times, the black woman has beenmade to wear the shame of humiliation, but because of her inner strength and a God that promises to deliver His people from all their afflictions, the black women could not be held down. Black women endured the anguish of having to suppress their desires of having fine homes and great entertainment, eating at famous resturants and wearing expensive clothing, while white women enjoyed all the flamboyancy of life. There were even times when the black women had to be the receipient of abuse by her own mate, and there was no one to come to her rescue. The black women had no rights in society and, in some occasions, no rights at home, yet still she learned to hold on to her dignity and continue to stand by her man. Black women prevailed.

Black women's struggles have always been different from that of white women's. White society encourages the success of white women, and, if anything at all, the system sometimes paint a negative picture of black men to black women, hence giving them more of a reason to cut the cords that bind them together as a unit. The role of black women must operate in the dimensions that include black men, and to ignore that responsibility would be like trying to establish a whole new different race. Men need women, and when they don't have them, they would try to create one, such as in the penal system, where some men are exploited to perform the function of women. Like wise, when there is no man in the life of a women, she will begin to assume the duties of one.

The role of the black women is critical in the rejuvenation and building of self-esteem in black men. Women are natural nurtures, and have the ability to influence the outcome of many situations in the lives of men; however, they must use wisdom and understanding to produce the kind of outcome that will benefit the black family unit. While men are moved by what they see, women are moved by what they hear, it is of the upmost importance that women hear the right words from their mates.

Imagine taking a hiking trip, with all the hills and valleys. Of course, you must cross the streams and rivers and be aware of visible as well as unseen dangers. Along the way, you lose a leg, then an arm, an ear...I guess by now you can see that it would be pretty hard for you to finish hiking. But if you give up, it's over. Women, you are on a hiking trip in a sense. Your legs may be your values, your arms may be your morals, and your ears may be your loyalty. If you lose any of these, it will be tough all the way to the end. So somewhere down the road you need to take a stand on quality, something that won't wear away in a few years. Make sure the man you let into your life has self-respect.

Jesus Christ said in a sermon: **"He who among you that is the greatest, shall be your servant" (Matt 20:26).**

If you want to be treated with love, respect, and dignity, you must learn to be all those in return, for we all reap what we sow.

Sometimes, the best way to see yourself is through the eyes of others. Constructive criticism has its place in our lives, and that is why most businesses that deal with the public have some questionnaire for you to grade them on their performance. It helps them to improve service to you. When we get right down to it, we find that you teach people how to treat you. When one is on the bottom, it is imperative that every step you take and every move you make are affirmative, because the spirit of failure, which is link to poverty and poor self-esteem, is always ready to push you back and hold you down. If black women want to see how organized evil work reveals itself, just look at what happened to Congresswoman Cynthia McKinney and the young black college student Crystal Gail Mangum, who was allegedly raped. It was a chance to see how society sympathized with the plight of the black women. It also revealed why it is so important to seek peace, for each of those incidents could have been avoided, simply by asking the question, "What if?" We are our brothers' keepers, and what we do affects the next person who comes along. A black woman can never fully be accepted outside of her race until she is totally accepted inside her race. That can only happen when black men and women learn to heal their hurts and pains together. When black women learn to accept the inner beauty of themselves, only then will they be able to experience the results of where outer beauty can lead them. The role of the black women is still needed and must never be abandoned.

Black women are more desirable, intelligent, and wealthier than ever before, according to Ebony article March 2001 by Charles Whitaker:

> In 1960, for example, only 3.3 percent of Black women held college degrees. Today, nearly 16 percent of Black women hold at least a bachelor's degree (compared to 15 percent of Black men).

Because of the income gap between black and white men in time past, white women had more time to spend with their children while they were growing up in their most impressionable years; and did a great job teaching their girls how to be ladies and their boys how to be men. The luxury of having the opportunity to spend that kind of quality time for the black woman was denied because it took two incomes to accomplish what our white brothers could do with one. Though quantity was improved in governing our abilities to purchase, quality was diminished in governing our abilities to nurture. The absence of timely and consistent nurturing has left a void that cannot be repaired by human intellect alone. Something has affected the will of many black women and caused them to loose their willingness to challenge the pains-taking journey of repairing broken relationships. It was that "rolling up the sleeves" kind of faith that was the bedrock of the civil rights movement, and through that path, we conquered many challenges. Somehow, we have allowed the very faith that worked for us to be boxed up and put away like old photos.

The negative impact on black people is staggering when the role of the black women is not met. One of the most important roles for black women is to stand by her man, but it does not relieve her of the responsibility to help steer the direction of their relationship, which first must be built upon a foundation of mutual respect. A big mistake that many black women make is to overlook their mate's disrespectful and negative attitude and view it as love, or they hold to the fallacy that they can change them later. Black women have a responsibility to show their men how to treat them and hold them to a much higher standard than in times past.

WHAT DOES " I DO" MEAN?

In marriage, when couples say "I do," have they really considered what it means to say it? If they do, why are there so many children in neighborhoods all over america living in single parent homes where there used to be two parents living there? It appears from all the divorces going on in this country today that nobody understands what "I do" means. Could it be that integrity is so weak that "I do" needs to be replaced with "I will try"? Instead of calling a marriage a covenant contract, maybe it should be called an "if it goes my way I'll stay" variable agreement.

The following is a reprint from divorcePeers.com:
- In 1998 2.2 million couples married and 1.1 million couples divorced.
- In 2000 58 million couples were married, yet separated.
- In 2000 there were over 21 million divorces.
- People between the ages of 25 to 39 make up 60% of all divorces.
- Over one million children are affected by divorce each year.
- Approximately 1/3 of divorced parents remain bitter and hostile several years after the divorce.
- In 1990 the average female age for re-marriage after divorce was 30.6 years; for males, 33.7 years of age.
- In 1990 the average female age for a second divorce was 37.3 years, for males, 40.4 years of age.
- More people are part of second marriages today than first marriages.

If you sign a contract to lease a car for a year and return it before the year is up, you will be held responsible for the complete term of the contract, but a marriage contract can be broken without the civil jeopardy, regardless of how much pain and suffering it causes.

"Do you take this person to be your lawful mate, to have and hold," meaning "to possess and cling to"? "Through sickness and health," meaning "whether you remain well or become ill." "For better or worse," meaning "if you are fifty rich or even dirt poor." "To love and cherish," meaning "to care for like as your own body and hold dear to your heart."

"Until death do you part," meaning just that. It seems that something is terribly wrong here, and I believe it has a great deal to do with accountablity; you see, everyone has the accountablity even if they don't take the responsibility.

"I do" means having the kind of redemptive heart and mind that will say, "I will stand upon the solid rock of truth, goodness, and justice to show that true love never fails nor loses its power." It means I know that you are not perfect, but together we can work towards perfection. It means together we stand, but divided we fall. It means what's important to you is also to me. It means that I will not give up on you or let you give up on yourself.

Jesus Christ said, " I will never leave you nor forsake you" and we must certainly adopt that same philosophy. It would be difficult for anyone to comprehend how important is to remain faithful unless you take time out and look at the whole process of life. It would be meaningless to have all that profoundness of being born and living some years and then just die. I believe that there is much more to life than that, and likewise, there is much more to marriage.

"I do" does not mean that when the path of marriage get crowded with challenges

that require some give and take, you turn around and go the other way. Many people are looked over for promotions on their jobs because of a refusal to overcome obstacles. The best place to learn how to be responsible is at home.

"I do" does not mean that just because you are recognized by society as owners of each other's interest that you can do or say whatever, whenever, wherever, and however you want to. You must understand that what ever life you live, it is the one that you created through the steps that you take and the moves you make. If it is not the one that you want, you can change it by mixing different kinds of ingredients for a different outcome.

Life skills are a must, but society has never taught in school how to prepare and be successful in one's morals. If these lessons are not taught at home, the television will have to be the teacher and most certainly do more harm than good.

"I do" means that I realize that it takes two in order to work together in harmony to achieve our goals, and that your desire is just as important as mine. It means that I need to understand and love you for who you are and not for who I want you to be. It means that when you can't go that extra mile, then I will go it for you.

"I do" means that I will give you space when you need it and be there to hold you when you feel lonely. It means that I will protect you and keep you free from harm and place no other person above you. It means that when you need help, I will be there and encourage you to be all that you can be.

WHAT ARE YOUR EXPECTATIONS?

Have you ever really taken the time and decided what you want out of life and the requirements needed to make those desires come true?

My soul, wait thou only upon God; for my expectation is from Him. He is my defense; I shall not be moved. In God is my salvation and my glory: the rock of my strength, and my refuge, is in God (Psalm 62:5-7).

Everyone has expectations, but meeting them is another matter. The Bible encourages us to have expectations and to depend on God to give us help in fulfilling those expectations. If you want to know about building a house, ask a carpenter; repairing a car, ask a auto mechanic; planting crops, ask a farmer; understanding life, ask God, for He is the creator of it; and if you want to know the purpose of a thing, ask the thing's maker. Expectation is not something that you establish on a whim, but rather time and consideration must be put into it, because it will be in the forefront of every decision you make; and those who ignore it will no doubt make many catastrophic mistakes.

The University of Waterloo career development manual gives six steps to success, which are self-assessment, research, decision-making, networks and contacts, work, life work and planning. All of those steps must be preceded by expectations, for where there are no expectations there will be no reason to look forward to anything in life. Expectations will cause a person to strive to achieve, and there have been so many issues in life that have hindered the efforts of many black men and deterred their expectations.

Everyone in life leaves a trail as they move from one stage to another, and because of that trail, we are able to know about the pros and cons of many decisions that were made. I have to wonder why we follow so many of the same trails that consistently proves to lead to destruction.

In the bible, Paul says, **for the good that I would I do not, but the evil which I would not, that I do. Now if I do that I would not, it is no more I that do it, but sin that dwelled in me (Roman 7:19-20).**

What Paul was saying is that the expectation that he wanted to express was hindered by a character flaw, so it was not that he desired not to convey it, but rather that the negative influence kept him from conveying it. We cannot ignore the fact that we make so many unwise decisions even when we know absolutely that they are the wrong ones to make.

Remember growing up? You probably did a lot of observation of how adults carried themselves. You probably said a lot of "I'm going to be this" and "I'm going to do that." You were developing your own expectations that you derived through interpretation of what you saw and heard. At first, you wanted to be everything, but as you grew older, you realized that you could not do it all and the time had come to decide about life. We take it upon our selves to choose and often bring the expectations of other people's opinions in our lives to a point that what they think becomes more important than what we think when it comes to our personal goals. When we are confused, we feel lonely and ready to give the helm of our lives to someone else to guide instead of learning to nurture our own plans.

Many get into trouble trying to live according to other people's expectations, and fear can have a lot to do with moving away from your own ideals and embracing those of another. The most compelling reason why it so important to meet expectations is the effect it has on one's emotional well-being. Disappointment penetrates deep in the soul and can leave a trail longer than any road you ever travel on. Preparation is our greatest defense against failure of any kind. It allows you to work with others as well as to stand- alone. It gives you a well of confidence to draw from in times of uncertainty. Preparation is the under-writer of expectation and will ensure your place in society. Never quit expecting, for it brings us excitement, hope, joy, peace, and love, which in return give life to achieve your goals.

We must realize that when we choose to incorporate ourselves with someone else, we form a company. Then it becomes the responsibility of the two to share expectations without the assistance of any negative outside influences. When you authenticate your relationship with another, you will be well served to follow what the Bible tells us, that you are no longer two, but the two become one. Once that happens, it is impossible to separate without taking a part of the other person with you, which will leave you physically and emotionally challenged. There is a force that is working against you, and the sooner you realize this the better off you will be. Perhaps you may be saying by now, "What kind of force is this nut talking about?" Well, the Bible teaches us that the war is not between flesh and blood, but principalities and power and spiritual wickeness in high places. For every thing there is a cause and effect; if something goes up, then someone or something had to send it up. If someone speaks, then someone or something had to influence that spoken word. The majority of the whole world is influenced by some form of belief system, according to an article in Religious & Tolerance.org, "33 percent of the world population are christians and 19.9 percent are muslims, 13.4 percent are hindus, 12.7 percent are non-religious and the rest consist of athiest, buddhist, new age and etc." The point is that people use some form of fate to help obtain their expectations. It can be the catalyst that is needed to pull you out of your jungle. If the expression "misery loves company" is ever true, take a look around, on the street corners, in the nightclubs, in parks, under bridges, and in many other places. What do you see? Birds of a feather flocking together. Surely we need to come together in a more positive way to help suport expectations. Everyone in the world has expectations, but there are many things in life that can have a negative or positive influence. Those influences could come from a person, place, or thing, which can sometimes cause a person to abandon their expectations, not because they don't have them any more, but because what causes discomfort in their lives can lead them to abandon reaching their goals. Some things can nurish your expectation, but there are things that can push them away.

Never keep company with people who are always negative about your goals. Anything in life can be learned, and most things are achievable through time and consistency. You must feed your expectation with the things that cause it to grow and make you feel good inside about your choices. There are people who are actors, business leaders, athletes, and doctors who may not look deserving of the part they play, but where you go in life is not based on how you look, but on how diligent you are in your pursuit. Expectations are the doorway that leads to reality, because it makes all things possible to the mind, and what the mind can believe, it also can achieve.

WHAT ARE YOUR RESPONSIBILITIES?

Responsibilities are like roads. There are many of them, long and winding, hilly, full of bridges, paved and unpaved. According to an article in wikipedia.org. People feel social responsibility, natural responsibility, and collective responsibility. Social responsibility allows for continued support to our society. We all benefit from that support to build schools, hospitals, libraries, roads, information systems, and much more, and these responsibilities are so vital that money is continually taken from our paychecks to ensure sustainability of these great needs. Natural responsibilities are self-implied rules that people follow to take care of others. This type of responsibility emanates from within one's self and cannot be taught, only enhanced through spending quite time alone. It can be seen through the faces of love, compassion, and empathy. Natural responsibility is what makes us logically care for one another and ourselves. The most important time in a person's life begins in the womb. It is where you receive all the nutriments necessary for life's journey, and no one else is in there to share or explain it to you. So being alone is a precious time and very much a requirement. Even when the drums of death come beating at your door, you have to go alone. Being alone can sometimes be a scary place, such as walking through a graveyard late at night or masking dark, shameful secrets, but also, to one's delight, it can be a place to shine in the solitude of hidden agendas. In our natural state we can master our natural responsibilities, which are to ensure that all of our faculties are working properly so we can be the best that we can be.

Wikipedia, the free encyclopedia, says "collective responsibility is a concept, or doctrine, according to which people are to be held responsible for other people's actions by tolerating, ignoring, or harboring them, without actively collaborating in these actions."

Many people are victims of collective responsibility, and because they give in to the peer pressure of groups, gangs, friends, or just getting caught up in the passion of the moment, a lot of lives have been destroyed. People will often do in a crowd what they would never do alone. It was the crowd that convinced the people to crucify Jesus. It was the crowd that became the catalyst that hung many Negroes during slavery and beyond. It is the crowd that keeps our young black men loyal to crime, violence, addictions, and failure.

Not all collective responsibility is negative. There are many good things that come from grouping together, for there is power in numbers. But one has to remember, whatever you tie yourself to is what you will become a part of.

Responsibilities are vital for you to be accountable. It gives you a sense of accomplishment, self-esteem, and success, and we need to take our responsibilities as seriously as a breath of air is to life. When things get difficult , that is the very time we need to stand, and after we have done all that we can do, continue to stand. I know we expect more out of life than we sometime get. All the promises and gonna do's seem just to vanish right before our eyes. It seems like the needs are endless, there are the "I needs", "he needs", "she needs", "baby needs" "car needs", "mom needs," and the list goes on and on, until finally the need to get away from it all.

It is important to reward yourself every now and then by doing something that makes you happy and joyful, because when you lose your joy, you lose hope. A hopeless person does not have anything to live for, and when you don't have any thing to live for, you also lose respect for all rules that govern responsibilities to yourself and to others. If we as black people do not take the responsibility of securing our future by first being responsible to ourselves, families, and each other, how can we expect anyone else to see us as somebody?

It is possible that everybody can be out for themselves, and nobody has anything; but it is impossible for everybody to be for each other and no one have anything.

In the Bible, **Psalm 121:1 "I lift up my eyes to the hills where my help comes from."**

The Lord is your hill. He is your help, and He still has His responsibilities and wants you to remember that He will never leave you nor forsake you.

Just because you have a flat tire on you car does not mean that you are going to throw away the car. No, you will fix the flat and continue on your way. You need not wait for someone to come and hand you a basket full of responsibilities; they are everywhere. When things go wrong, that is the time to stop and go back to the beginning, the basics. Most of the time when life's problems are over-shadowing us, it's because at the beginning we fail to see or do something. All things can be worked out to a degree that can be tolerable for all parties involved. It will take someone willing to be responsible and a desire to see a positive outcome for all. There are a lot of children who have been abandonned because someone failed to be responsible, and really, a child is you, only just at a different place and time. Many psychologists will tell you the effects of family separation on children. According to an article in Family Life Facts by Dr. Tod E, Linaman, "Only acts of war and the events of natural disasters are more harmful to a child's psyche than the divorce process." *The Newsletter of the American Academy of Matrimonial Lawyers*, summer 1997:

- Social science research reveals that the effects of divorce not only impact a child into adulthood, but they also affect the next generation of children as well.
- Children from divorced families drop out of school at twice the rate of children from intact families.
- The single best predictor of teen suicide is parental divorce and living in a single parent household.
- Children of divorced parents are significantly more likely to become delinquent by age 15, regardless of when the divorce took place, than are children whose own parents are married.
- Comparing all family structures, drug use in children is lowest in the intact married family.

- Children whose parents divorce have lower rates of graduation from high school and college and also complete fewer college courses.
- Children from divorced homes performed more poorly in reading, spelling, and math and repeated a grade more frequently than did children from intact two-parent families.
- The college attendance rate is about 60 percent lower among children of divorced parents compared with children of intact families.
- Divorce has been found to be associated with a higher incidence of depression, withdrawal from friends and family; aggressive, impulsive, or hyperactive behavior; and either withdrawing from participation in the classroom or becoming disruptive.
- Adult children of divorced parents experience mental health problems significantly more often than do the adult children of intact families.
- Children younger than five years of age are found to be more vulnerable to the emotional conflicts occurring during the separation and divorce of their parents. Older children frequently withdraw from home life and seek intimacy away from home.
- If divorce occurs when the children are teenagers (12 to 15 years of age), they tend to react in two very different ways: by attempting to avoid growing up or by attempting to "speed through" adolescence.
- Teenagers also tend to experience increased aggression, loss of self-confidence, and loneliness. Boys are more likely to be depressed than girls.
- The child's suffering does not reach its peak at the time of the divorce and then level off. Rather, the emotional effects of the parents' divorce can be played and replayed throughout the next three decades of a child's life".

After reading that kind of data on the impact that a lack of responsibility can produce, how can one not hold one's head down in shame and cry out for another chance to make it right? The most wonderful part about a second chance is the joy that comes with restoring that light that has gone out of a child's future. There are many black children whose lives are being destroyed because the ones who are responsible for their births fail to be responsible for their lives after birth. It should be very clear who is destroying the black race.

ARE YOU FACING THE TRUTH?

Webster's defines truth as the facts corresponding with actual events or happenings, sincerity, or honesty. Have you ever told a lie and had it lay heavily on your mind? What about if it never bothered your conscience at all? Well, to be perfectly honesty about it, the truth is not based on how you feel, or what you do, but rather the facts qualify truth. Many people ask whether truth is subjective, relative, objective, or absolute. An article on truth in Wikipedia mentions that "Friedrich Nietzsche believed the search for truth or 'the will to truth' was a consequence of the will to power of philosophers. He thought that truth should be used as long as it promoted life and the will to power, and he thought untruth was better than truth if it had this life enhancement as a consequence." Now that kind of philosophy appears to be prevalent in our society, especially in areas that are affected greatly by drugs, gangs, unemployment, and violence. When truth is subjective to feelings and where there are no absolutes, truth becomes relative to strength, power, money and fear. The wrong information is much more negative than no information at all. There are many black brothers and sisters who are suffering because of wrong information that cannot possibly lead to the truth. They are being spoon-fed that all problems are from the white establishment, so the only way to gain true freedom is to dismantle the white establishment. This kind of thinking says that as long as white people are in charge of a certain thing, then black people can never be free. So many black brothers and sisters feel victimized and inadequate in their abilities. This lie feeds into the notion that you are down because you are being held by the white system, and there is no need to believe that hard work, planning, and following through will get you anywhere in life. Truth will tell you that what you put in is what you get out, and you shall reap what you sow. It tells you that whatever you focus on, you will be drawn towards it, and no one can stop you but you. The truth will give you responsibility, but a lie will take it away and leave your life to chance. When you face the truth, you can look opposition straight in the face and say, "Be it as it may, but I'm going to do my best and expect the best to happen for me; and I won't change, but I will wait for my chance to come." When the truth comes out, you will find much opposition to its presence, because it exposes the lie and whoever tells it. There have been so many people obstracized, hurt, or killed trying to protect a lie that can never be truly concealed. What ever benefits that can come from a lie, the truth can be much more beneficial than a lie could possibly be. The truth will uncover failure, poverty, and crime and allow you to see just how amazing you really are. It will enable you to know your God-given potential and how to tap into it. Truth will encourage you to navigate your life based on your desires and not by what you see or feel, nor what others may think of you. If black people who are living in dispair would first face the truth and then enbrace it, they would see that truth really can set you free. Truth is great, and greatness belongs to all who desire it. Society has created a mold that categorizes people based on their educational level and gives more credence to those who are the so-called experts based on their degrees; but whether you have a degree or not, where you go in life is based on where you stand with your desires. Many people have degrees and are still living in poverty, and there are those who have not finished high school and yet are millionaires.

In the world of electricity, current takes the path of the least resistance; but in the world of life, the path of least resistance often only leads to failure. Things that come quickly are usually associated with losing. It can take years to build something, but minutes to tear it down. It takes years to live, but seconds to die. What keeps a plane afloat is the fact that it is moving, but if if stops moving, it will surely crash, and as a plane was designed to move forward, so is the truth also design to take you forward. As black people, we can't afford to refuse to acknowledge that there are problems in our culture in the areas of education, sexual identity, crime, drug abuse, self-esteem, speaking properly, and many other things. There are those who resist the need to strive for excellence and refuse to acknowledge they have some challenges; when they are corrected or given constructive feedback, they turn on the broken record that plays the song, "It's Because I'm Black." When you accept the truth, you learn first to look at yourself and ask if it's possible that you could be portraying a negative impression. You must understand that you have the power to change and rearrange your situation anywhere, place, or time. The ability to excel is everywhere in the black culture; no matter what part of town you may have grown up in, there are always success stories. The truth is that even if a criminal took their energy, boldness, and determination and used it to start a legitimate business, they would be successful. There are many blacks all over the world who decided to embrace the truth and not live their lives through the eyes of other people, but instead, allowed the truth to show they could achieve anything they desired, and that if they believed in themselves, others had no choice but to believe in them also. Failure operates on the wheels of lies, but success moves by the force of truth. In one move, truth will punish the evil and free the guilty conscience.

When we as black people face the truth, we won't focus on what color we are, nor the color of anyone else, but rather, we will see ourselves as human beings, equal as all other races. While facing the truth, we will find that there are still a lot of stigmas that people will want to attach to us, but we do not have to be who they say we are, or do what they say we do, but we can be proud of who we are and be disciplined enough to follow through with our goals. The truth is that often the only difference between a rich man and a poor man is that the rich man is disciplined. There are many people who have lost their dreams and goals not because they lack the ability, but because they lack the discipline it takes to reach their goal. Discipline is not just being punished for something that you did wrong. Discipline is also what pushes you to do something right.

Every black man should be willing to contribute towards the continuity of our race. This can be done by first facing the truth that you are either adding or taking away from a positive perception of who we are as black people. We must realize that when one person commits a crime, the whole race suffers from it in one way or another; no one is choiceless when it comes to deciding on which path to take.The truth is that we all have a choice in every decision that confronts us. Which one will you make? Blacks have been gifted with a strong foundation by black pioneers such as Harriet Tubman, Fredrick Douglass, Denmark Vessey, George Washington Carver, Thomas L. Jennings, Martin Luther King, Malcom X, and many others who have helped black people to see injustice and face the truth of our abilities to do something about them.

There are many wealthy blacks who have the means to make an enormous impact in the black communities, but to be fair about it, we cannot expect them to deplete all they have worked for or blessed enough to abtain on behalf of our race. On the other hand, not enough of them are willing to part with their money, even though their wealth is more than that of communities in some cases. If a person makes forty thousand dollars a year, it would take twenty-five years to make one million dollars. So many wealthy black people make more money in six month than most people make in forty years. When they get caught up in greed rather than need, then they are forever chasing the love of money over the love of fellow man. In the Bible **1 Timothy 6:10, "For the love of money is the root of all evil: which while some coveted after, they have erred from the faith, and pierced themselves through with many sorrows."** When our love of money becomes more powerful than our desire to help one another, you lose the truth that money is a means to fulfill responsibilities and allowing the benefit of reaping what you have sown. To hand out money indiscriminately is not the answer, but it can help build an awareness foundation where people can better understand how to apply themselves. Truth can bring joy if you accept it early, but it also can bring sorrow if you accept it too late. The truth is that many black families are not taking truth seriously enough, for truth will tell you if you are spending money wisely, saving money for retirement, teaching your children how to save, investing time and energy with your family, or keeping company with the wrong crowd, and if you are walking in blessings or curses. The best way to be knowledgeable and free from lack, need, poverty, sin, and failure is to embrace truth, for you shall know the truth and the truth shall make you free.

LIFE POEM TRUTH

© By JOSEPH E. APONTE JR

I CAN MAKE YOU SAD,
I CAN MAKE YOU MAD, AND SOMETIMES I'M THE BEST FEELING YOU EVER
HAD....
WHO AM I? I AM THE TRUTH.

I CAN SEND YOU TO HEAVEN...
OR, I CAN SEND YOU TO HELL.
I CAN'T BE TOUCHED NOR CAN I BE SMELLED.
WHO AM I? I AM THE TRUTH.

RESPECT ME OR HATE ME.
REJECT ME OR TAKE ME.
REPRESENT ME OR FAKE ME.
I'LL ALWAYS REMAIN THE ALMIGHTY TRUTH.

DEVELOPING A NEW ATTITUDE

The key term here is "new attitude," which is another way of saying "a second chance by your own discretion." It is yours for the taking, but it's up to you to develop it. In Recovery Medicine dot Com, an article by Irene Segal said "The way you think, day in day out, affects all aspects of your life. Learning to listen to your 'internal dialogue' will help you recognize your thought patterns and how they may be affecting the way you handle the stressful situations of daily living." Many people would say that if you talk to yourself, you must be crazy, but I say if you do not talk to yourself, you must be crazy. Everyone has an internal dialogue going on, and when you ignore it, that won't make it go away. It is there to help you think things through, because most people get into trouble when they don't think things through. When a person doesn't see the real benefit of learning how to develop things, the lack of that understanding will lead to a stressful and undesirable life. Many great ideals and bright futures have been left behind or died because people did not know how to move their thoughts from an infant state to maturity. Society is set up to develop you externally, but it must be your personal efforts that develop you internally. To be successful in developing a new attitude, you first must conquer fear. Fear plays a part in your life in small increments sometimes unnoticeable in the present situation. One of the most common fears is that of being alone, leading many to choose to be with failure rather than be alone. It takes a mind that is willing to step up to the plate and say, "I must make this decision because it is my responsibility." Many people attach themselves to gangs, hangouts, groups, and unproductive people because they do not want to be alone. When they are with a group, the group makes the decisions for them and they are off the hook from making a choice and being responsible. A person must first realize that they need to change before they can have a new attitude. There will be times when it seems like the change that you are seeking is not worth the time and effort. The change will come with demands and sacrifices and rules, just as when a person goes into the military and enters boot camp to push out the old way and bring in the new way that will prepare them to succeed in their new life. The Bible says in **Matthew 9:17, "Neither do men put new wine into old bottles: else the bottles break, and the wine runs out, and the bottles perish: but they put new wine into new bottles, and both are preserved."** In other words, it will be difficult to put a new attitude into an old way of life; a new attitude needs a new willingness, a new desire, and a new platform in order to be successful. A new attitude must come out from among them and be separated so it can properly be transformed into the new man or woman; it also must be exercised and utilized so that familiarity can set in. The attitude is the soil that every decision grows out of, and if the attitude is poor, the decision will be poor, but if the attitude is rich with excitement and hope, the decision will reflect the same.

The black family will find it difficult to emerge into the twenty-first century with an optimistic view unless it leaves behind the old victim mentality. A victim's outlook produces a dark heart full of rage and bitterness and inhibits a full integration into society's mainstream. It justifies not trying by saying that if you are black, you won't get it regardless of how well prepared you are. Too many qualified blacks give up before they ever get started, because in their minds, everything belongs to the white man, so they feel disqualified and refuse to put forth consistent effort from the start.

Any group of people who have endured and come out of over four hundred years of slavery should believe that nothing could be withheld from them. It took more than being just a man to have endured the hardness of slavery; it took something so deep down profound that words could never be able to explain the reality of it.

Out of the suffering of Jesus Christ came eternal life in the spirit, and so it also must be that out of the suffering of the black race comes life in the flesh. The debt was paid so that you may feel qualified to move forward into the abundant life of this nation. We must not move from being enslaved by men to being enslaved by the attitude that put a noose of drugs, violence, sex, and failure around our necks from which to be hanged until dead. We must wake up men of valor, honor, and integrity to shout from the mountaintops and to the valleys below that we are more than able to prosper in the land.

Attitudes develop situations. Situations must be created and do not have a life of their own, but attitude is a creator, and can create or destroy. The first responders of attitude patrollers are black men. They all are accountable, but not all are responsible, and one thing that is certain, whoever they are, wherever they are, they must answer through the life they and their children live.

The church should be a brain center where a person can get in touch with a support group for an attitude change. It must be looked at as a place where you can learn how to, but the practice will be at home and abroad. The pastors of congregations may or may not be in line themselves, but the word itself is always true, for it does not come from man, only through him. The word of God itself is designed to open up doors of understanding that could never be revealed without the anointed intervention of God's purpose. More lives have been changed through the relationship of man with God than men with men according to Gods abilities verses men. The attitude of God teaches us how to deal with the attitude of men, and the closer we stick to the rules the more effective we will become. There are more assistants to do wrong than help to do right. Supporting the pathways that lead to doing what is right in life requires rules to keep the integrity and pureness of the way. Chaos is that which is abstract and out of order and can never lead to purpose and destiny. Attitude will either qualify or disqualify you to handle success in life. How you feel about something is just as important as the thing itself. The black family unit is only as strong as the parts of the unit, and the black man is responsible for ensuring the unit is held together, but he can only be a leader when he has the ability to lead. To lead should be an honor worthy of preparing for, and that preparation should take place from the age of birth. When a corporation falls, it's because of poor leadership, and when a family falls, it's because of a poor leader. When there is failure in a relationship, the problem is not with the relationship or the people. The people are fine, but their attitudes are not. You cannot adjust people, but you can adjust attitudes.

The black family cannot afford to settle for less than what its capabilities are. They must remain optimistic about the future and the course of this nation. They must see themselves as viable and integral to the fixing of the world's problems. The black family must not languish in the hurtful past of slavery and second-class citizenship. This unity cannot be achieved by black men marching; it can only be accomplished through non- violence, a, intimate relationship with peace, and a new attitude that will say, "I will no longer rob, kill, steal, or mistreat my brother, and I will respect, uphold, support, and love my sister. I will take my place in society and live off diligence and not excuses, and I will above all things walk in integrity."

CROSSING THE BRIDGE

To understand the urgency of the moment, one has only to drive or walk the streets of many of our black communities to see why black men and women should cross the bridge and come together. It sometimes seems as though we have lost our ability to see reality and face issues. Why are we allowing our lives and the future of our children be destroyed? Crossing the bridge will lead to freedom; it took Moses to cross the Red Sea in order to get to the Promised Land. We must leave behind the old way and take up the new way. The old way feeds negative outlooks with doom and gloom. It is an enemy to hope, dreams, goals, and positive inspirations in life. We must cross that bridge so when the walls of our minds begin to close in, we can hold firm to our understanding and stand up to the voices of destruction. If we don't know how to decipher mixed emotions, our life will stay in a zone of confusion. Crossing the bridge is the transition of moving away from the controlling diseases of need, low self-esteem, poverty, addictions, history, failure, divorce, and pride. These things will execute a level of control in your life that will hinder you from enjoying all that life has to offer. The black race must not carry the ball and chains of the past, no more than a divorced person should live their life in the shadows of a past relationship. Self-fulfilling prophecy plays too much of a role in the lives of the black race. The black race must not be the negative stereotype cliché that epitomizes us based on any infraction. We must not condone any ill behavior that is not excused by illness. Corruption cannot exist in our communities, unless the people of the community tolerate it. We must not allow the diseased infestation of attitudes to cross over and contaminate the new efforts.

There will be those fake leaders who will try to police every effort of inspired people who will tell it like it is, but those fake leaders only ridicule solutions because they have none of their own. If we as a black race are to cross the bridge, then we must not embrace leaders who separate us from other races of this nation and influence us to create our own world. It is true that one can get followers to do just about anything, from planting flowers to robbing banks. If you ask enough people, someone will agree with you. When a person is ready to cross the bridge, their mind is made up, and it does not matter if they benefit from Affirmative Action or their own action. All they know is that if there is a will, then there is a way, and they will find it. Affirmative Action programs were a tool to help minorities get jobs where otherwise would have been impossible. On the other hand, we must know that regardless of the benefits we receive from such programs, they don't last forever. That kind of awareness will prepare a person to walk with a level of understanding that will navigate them through whatever obstacles come their way and know that a prepared mind is a ready mind.

Crossing the bridge is really a means for connections. It is a way to network and bridge ideals and efforts to create a better approach. The black race as a whole lacks the right kind of connection with the right kind of people. There are too many black men still stuck in an identity crises by still trying to find out what to call themselves or what is accepted or not. There are no lasting satisfactions when some black men are moving forward through the gifts of athletic abilities while many others are still struggling to finish high school. We must tap into the desire and need to hold one another accountable to maximizing our efforts. We must not allow classisms to erode away our unity and separate us by those who have and those who have not. The ideal of being our brother's keeper must start at the time of adolescence, and we must not so easily give up on our brothers who have gone astray. The black race must set high standards and paint a clear picture of what is acceptable behavior, not turn the other way when crime began to manifest in our neighborhoods. Crossing the bridge says that you have packed up everything that you will need to make it on the other side and you are equipped to handle every situation. There are some situations that take place in our communities that cannot be corrected by one individual and will require the assistance of every able-bodied man in the community. We can network in a manner that will drive out the hoods, drug dealers, and gang-bingers to make the area pro-family. There are too many instances where the disobedient child winds up controlling and holding the community at bay while the good people are afraid to speak out. The only way that a gang can control a whole community is when the community refuses to unite. We owe it to our children to give them a safe and productive community to grow up in. Our churches also must learn how to cross the bridge by striving to be in touch with the community just as they seek to be in touch with God. The real effectiveness of your relationship with God is gauged through your usefulness throughout your communities. All too often our leaders are more interested in making an impact in their wallet than in their community. If they used the platform they have to bring the people to work together, there would be a great change throughout our communities. **Genesis 11: 6, "And the Lord said, behold, the people is one, and they have all one language; and this they begin to do; and now nothing will be restrained from them, which they have imagined to do."** The word of God tells us that we can accomplish anything when we come together, but when we are divided, our communities will also be that way, and our children will have a difficult time working in unity with others. Crossing the bridge can bring unity, just as when the black family crossed the ocean together in times of slavery. We had no choice but to stick together. Today, we have the opportunity to reach out to, care for, and encourage one another to be all that we can be. Success is open to those who can see themselves walking in it and belongs to whoever has a desire to go for it. We as black people can set the bar of excellence for our children to follow, and if we would walk in the abilities we have and hold our brothers and sister accountable to do the same, our future will be as bright and promising as any other race.

In the current Presidential campaign, Senator Obama is trying to bridge the divide that keeps all races of people estranged. One of the greatest obstacles in his way lies with the media, where people's jobs depend on how much confrontation they can cause and the media seizes every opportunity. Obama Pastor Jeremiah Wright spoke what was the truth, but the truth is what people really do not want to hear, especially at an inconvenient time. In our pursuit of victory, let us not forget to use prudence in our judgments knowing that God is ultimately the one and only true judge and when that day of judgment comes, every knee shall bend, every head shall bowed and every tongue shall confess.

WORK CITED

American Academy of Matrimonial Lawyers (*news letter 1997*) aaml.org

Aponte, Joseph E. JR. *Life Poem Truth*, Poemsabout.com

Bennett, Kinnon, *Can A Sister Get A Break*, Nov 23,2004 Highbeam.com

Bianchi 1995 *Grand Parents Maintains families*, US Bureau of Census.gov

BBC News *Driving While Black* April 2006 irr.org.uk

Center For American Progress *Population race*, americanprogress. org

Childress, Clinard H. JR, *Abortion In The Black Community*, Black Genocide.Org

DiIulio, John J, *My Black Crime Problem Divorce* Peers.Com

Dr Todd E. Linaman, *Effect of Divorce on children and families*, Family Life Facts.org

Holy Bible (King James Version)

Nietzsche, Friedrick, *What is Truth* Wikipedia.org

Rasberry, William, *Show Blacks How To Fill their glasses* April 11, 2005 Washington Post.com

Tolerance and Prayer in School, Religious & Tolerence.Org

Whitaker, Charles. *The Changing Role of Black Women,* March 2001, findarticle.com

Wikipedia.Org Single Parents

University of Waterloo, (Career Development Manuels) university of waterloo.edu

www.ingramcontent.com/pod-product-compliance
Lightning Source LLC
Chambersburg PA
CBHW050337290526
45785CB00006B/2526